EVERYTHING A GIRL
SHOULD KNOW

EVERYTHING A GIRL SHOULD KNOW

ABOUT: HEALTH, HAIR, SKIN, CLOTHES, PERIODS, SELF-CONFIDENCE

Samantha Rugen

Piccadilly Press · London

Phototypeset by Goodfellow and Egan, Cambridge
Printed and bound by WBC, Bridgend, Mid Glam.
for the publishers, Piccadilly Press Ltd.,
5 Castle Road, London NW1 8PR

A catalogue record for this book is available
from the British Library

ISBN: 1 85340 287 7 (H/back)
      1 85340 282 6 (T.p/back)

Samantha Rugen is a young Liverpudlian illustrator. She has
just completed a teacher training course. This is her first book.

CONTENTS

When you reach adolescence
your life isn't fair.
Your grease glands go wild
and you sprout lots of hair!
Your vest doesn't fit . . .
and your oestrogen surges,
you're covered in spots
then get sexual urges!
Then along comes the bra,
deodorant and razor
and you'll suddenly notice
a change of behaviour.
As your hormones calm down
you'll soon discover
that being a teenager
really wasn't a bummer!

by Samantha Rugen

Chapter One

HEARTY, HEALTHY, HAPPY YOU

EAU DE SURVIVAL

Your body is a finely tuned, extremely complex machine. It takes a lot of tender loving care to run it problem-free for 24 hours a day, 365 days a year and for 80-odd (usually) years, non-stop! It is made up of two-thirds water and it loses a few pints daily

through you sweating and going to the loo, which need to be replaced regularly. It is actually possible to survive without food for weeks, but you will only last a matter of days without water. Water also helps to give you a clear complexion and is extremely good for the system as it flushes all the poisons (or toxins) away. Try to drink at least several glasses of pure water a day.

SLEEPING BEAUTY

Sleep is another very important factor in staying healthy. As a teenager, you may find that you need more sleep than any other age group. You are tired because you are growing both physically and emotionally, at a rapid rate. If you are lucky, and your family let you sleep in, enjoy the luxury. You should aim to have at least seven to eight hours every night, but teenagers who have discovered a social life or study late into the night may be inclined to neglect their bodies' needs. The next day they are:

- irritable
- unable to concentrate
- slow-reflexed
- depressive
- moody

and unflattering black rings will develop under red puffy eyes, which will look far from attractive! Sleep is the closest thing your body gets to having a rest. It enables it to 'shut down' so that:

- muscles relax
- skin can renew itself
- heart rate slows down
- breathing becomes shallow
- reflexes and pain cease almost completely
- brain activity slows but does not stop entirely, causing every person to experience two or three dreams a night.

COUNTING SHEEP

Some people find it difficult to sleep and insomnia can be very frustrating. If you have this problem avoid chocolate, coffee or cheese near bedtime. Coffee and chocolate contain a stimulant which will keep you awake. Cheese is high in fat so it is not easily digested and the body carries on working longer to burn it off; this can also give you nightmares. Avoid heavy meals or strenuous exercise before bed too as your body will be stimulated to digest food or revved up from the exercise. If you have been studying late, try to have a relaxing routine afterwards to allow you to unwind.

Captivating Clichés
'It is best always to have a glass of hot milk to help
you sleep.'
   This is in fact true, although it might not work for
everyone.

HINTS FOR PERFECT DREAMS
If you still have problems getting to sleep, try one
of these:

- Read a book, preferably a boring one that will be easy to put down.
- Have a hot bath to help you relax. Add a drop of lavender oil to the water for a quicker effect.
- Do yoga or other relaxation exercises, such as taking deep breaths and slowly letting the air out.
- Think of every individual muscle from your toes upwards beginning to relax.
- Count sheep – or boys! (but that could well have the opposite effect!)
- Don't worry about not being able to sleep. This will only keep you awake even longer!

If you *still* have no success, see your doctor. There are also some very good homeopathic remedies which may help.

FOOD FOR THOUGHT

Looking after yourself should also include watching yourself when it comes to eating. If you want to look good, you must eat well. This means regularly eating a balanced diet with a selection of healthy food. Three square meals a day really is the best.

It's important to have a diet with plenty of nutritional value – things which tend to be eaten as snacks (sweets, crisps etc) don't have much, so you shouldn't snack your way through the day at the expense of eating properly.

For a balanced diet you should have something from each of the following groups every day:

- meat, fish or alternatives like beans, rice, nuts
- milk and dairy products (cheese, yoghurt)
- bread, cereals, pasta
- vegetables
- fruit

Eliminating even one of these groups from your diet means that you are not eating properly.

DIETING

Thousands of women fight the battle of the (often non-existent) bulge, many for their whole lives. Women often feel pressurised to be as perfect as the images the media spread everywhere. Usually there is little or no reason for teenagers to lose weight. Remember, there is such a thing as puppy fat; you may be unhappy with your size now, but as you grow taller you become slimmer naturally. Having said that, a lot of people are overweight. If you do go on a diet, you must be careful:

1) The Deadly Diet.
Because food is a major cause for concern with many young girls, serious diseases like anorexia nervosa and bulimia are quite common. These diseases quite often begin life as seemingly-innocent diets, which then turn into an obsession with food. Anorexia nervosa involves convincing yourself that you are fat, although most victims are very thin. It can lead to hospitalisation and a very long process of recuperation, if not death. Bulimia involves bingeing on food but keeping the weight down in two ways: (i) by inducing vomiting so the food never reaches the stomach and (ii) by taking laxatives so the food will go straight through without having time to be digested. This can also lead to hospital treatment. Often those suffering from anorexia (as it is commonly called) become bulimic and the reverse can also be true.

7

Captivating Clichés
'*Once you have been on a diet, you put all the weight back on again and more.*'

If you do go on a crash diet such as the 'drink a milkshake', 'take a tablet', or 'eat prunes for three weeks' diets, then this is likely to be true. Crash diets prevent the body getting the nutrients it really needs. When you begin to eat normally again, the body stores them in case of any future emergencies, in the form of fat.

2) The Ultimate Diet.
The only sure way to lose weight is to eat less, but sensibly, and take plenty of exercise. Cut out sugary or fatty foods, which are often eaten as snacks, and have lots of fruit and vegetables instead. Cut down on the amount of red meat you eat and stick to white meat and fish instead (if you are a vegetarian of course, this will not apply to you). If you can combine sensible eating with lots of healthy exercise (like swimming, walking or exercise classes), you will feel the extra pounds melt away. You can practically starve yourself but still have flabby bits which need toning up.

Do remember that you may be the right size anyway. Look at your family. You may have inherited 'big bones' (a large frame) or a propensity to carry more weight than you like. Don't make yourself miserable just because you aren't wafer

thin. The most attractive people in the world are active, healthy, energetic people, and some of those are what the media would call 'overweight'.

ON YOUR BIKE – EXERCISE

Exercise is a vital part of healthy living and is usually a compulsory part of every teenager's school timetable. However, a few gym lessons a week is really not enough and it is a good idea to take exercise outside school as well – the more the better! Aerobics and step classes can be a good choice for the less sporty teenager, and there are hundreds of other activities to choose from. If you are spoilt for choice, try swimming; it is an excellent overall form of exercise and is reputed to use every muscle in the body. Cycling is also excellent, and has the added bonus of being a cheap and independent way of getting around too.

Also try to take some exercise in the fresh air every day, even if it is just walking. This avoids that pallid, unhealthy look that comes from being inside all day.

THREE TEMPTATIONS THAT COULD BE SINS: ALCOHOL, DRUGS AND SMOKING

Teenagers should know as much as possible about these three 'sins'.

ALCOHOL

Of the adult population, ninety per cent consume alcohol on a regular basis. Although it is illegal to drink in public under the age of 18, most people have tried it at home in their early teens. Always have your first taste of alcohol with your parents if possible. A little drop of wine in your water when

you and your parents think it appropriate is a good
way of discovering what it tastes like. Alcohol can
take effect very quickly depending on:

- whether you have eaten recently
- how much you have drunk
- how often you drink
- how quickly it is taken
- your body weight

As a teenager, your body is unused to alcohol, so its
effects can be particularly startling. Alcohol in
moderation can make you feel relaxed and happy.
In excess, you may become uncoordinated, slur
your words, lose balance easily, vomit or even pass
out! You might also do and say things which in
normal circumstances you wouldn't. Those things
can come back to haunt you too! If you are thinking
of drinking in the future, always have something to
eat or a glass of milk beforehand – and drink at your
own pace. Drinking water afterwards will help stop
dehydration which is the cause of hangovers.

DRUGS

Drugs might make you feel better momentarily, but
they can give you long-term problems, particularly
the addictive ones. They can also make you broke –
because they are illegal, they are expensive. You
would be better spending your money on
something worthwhile. Make certain that you

11

understand and know about the different sorts of
drugs and their effects.

SMOKING

There is a drug more commonly used and widely
accepted than any other, that causes over 100,000
premature deaths in this country alone every year –
tobacco – and most people start smoking it in their
teens. Tobacco is a legal drug used by 38 per cent of
the population. It is supposed to:

- reduce appetite
- stop anxiety and stress
- relax you

It is also highly addictive, very expensive and
harmful both to those who smoke and those around

them. There is growing evidence that even passive smokers can suffer the same diseases (mainly involving heart and lung problems) through no fault of their own, so if your parents or anyone else you know smoke, you can tell them that.

In some circles, there is pressure on teenagers to smoke, drink, or take drugs in order to look good and 'cool'. Remember, you are the 'coolest' when you know *you* – what you want and what you don't want and are able to stick to your views in spite of possible disagreements and pressure otherwise. Your friends should respect you and your wishes. If they don't, then they aren't your friends!

Perhaps you don't care what alcohol, drugs and smoking do to your insides; after all, you can't see them. But just think what they do to your looks. Alcohol in excess causes broken veins, blotchy skin and is a sure way to put on weight. Smokers have stained teeth, their skin ages quicker, they have dreadfully smelly breath which isn't attractive to anyone. Drugs can absolutely ruin your looks, especially as you can become so dependent on them that all that matters is when you can have more drugs, and you don't care what you look like by then.

Chapter Two

PERIODS – NO PROBLEM

PERIODS – THE SCARY WORD

The mere mention of the word 'period' can make many girls cringe. Even when it is reworded into some kind of code like 'having the painters in', 'being on', 'starting' or 'the curse' there is no escaping the embarrassment. However this is all uncalled for. Talking about this 'miracle of nature' should not be taboo as about 50 per cent of the population experience them. When you actually consider what is happening 'down there' every four weeks or so, you should be bragging and making the opposite sex jealous. Their bodies don't allow them to produce another human being! (If they did, you could be sure that the subject of MENstruation (periods) would be their only topic of conversation!)

During the 1800s, the average age for a girl to start having periods was 17, today, because of improved diet, it is 12. During your lifetime you will have somewhere between 300 and 500 periods which will last between two and ten days each and occur every 20 to 40 days.

BLAME IT ON THOSE HOR-MOANS

What exactly is happening? Blame your hormones. During puberty they appear from nowhere and go berserk! Your uterus, which is right up inside your body, prepares for a baby. Whether or not you want one doesn't matter! This means that your body releases an egg from your fallopian tubes which travels down towards your uterus in the hope that it will meet and be fertilised by a male sperm. If all goes according to plan, then it has a cosy home for nine months. If, however, the two do not meet for some reason, because, for instance, you have not had sex or you have but you used a form of contraception correctly, then you will have a period. This involves the uterus once again. As it has been patiently waiting for the fertilised egg, it realises it has been wasting its time and sheds the lining the egg would have been embedded in. This is seen in the form of blood which is not always the bright red you would expect.

THE FIRST TIME

So, have you started yet? This waiting game can be a traumatic time for many girls who feel left behind from this thing called 'womanhood'. If you feel that your hormones are incapable of doing anything

other than producing spots, then do not worry.
This is actually serious medical advice. Stress can
play havoc with a girl's body and delay
menstruation. It will usually happen sooner rather
than later, but if you do reach 16 or 17 and are still
concerned, see a doctor. (Stress continues to play a
role in your cycle throughout life. It can often delay
periods or even bring them on.)

Your first period will probably be brown, and in

17

the future, at the beginning and end of your period, the flow will be light and so will also appear brown. The first few periods may even stop, then restart a day or so later. Once you have started, your periods will take a while to settle down and get into a predictable routine. That means you may not know your own exact cycle for some time.

BE PREPARED

As all Girl Guides should know, their motto is 'be prepared'. It should also be every teenage girl's, as it is helpful advice regarding periods. Always try to carry around some form of sanitary protection as you never know when you may be caught unawares, even if you haven't started yet. Try not to rely on the machines in ladies' loos. How often do they work and do you think you would really have the right change to put in the slot?

Often the first period is a little unexpected. As girls usually start between the ages of 10 and 16, then it is pretty difficult to predict! Don't worry too much. A first period tends to be very light, especially for the first day, so you are unlikely to leak. If you have started your periods and you think your next one is about to begin, wear a 'mattress', as even the smallest leak on clothing can be highly embarrassing. It is definitely better to be safe rather than sorry.

IT'S MY LIFE – DIFFERENT FORMS OF SANITARY PROTECTION

What form of protection should you use? You only have to look in a chemist to be bombarded with a huge selection of brands, sizes and forms. They range from the 'super deluxe press-on' to the 'teeny weeny panty liner' and from 'Niagara Falls heavy flow tampon with cardboard applicator' to 'microscopic applicator-free tampon'. The choice is yours!

SANITARY TOWELS – 'MATTRESSES'

For your first period it is probably sensible to use a towel/'pad'/'mattress'. There is very little fiddling around involved in putting it on which is lucky as you are likely to be in a bit of a flap anyway! You simply tear off the backing strip and stick it into your knickers. There is a knack to getting it in the right position so it feels comfortable, but you will learn that very quickly.

Manufacturers suggest that you change towels every three to four hours but you may find this is too long. If you feel uncomfortable then it probably needs changing. Don't leave it on for much longer than the recommended time otherwise you may begin to notice an unpleasant smell wafting round or embarrassing leaks could occur. Disposing of 'mattresses' is a very straightforward process. If you're at home then either wrap it up and drop it into a wastebasket or tear it lengthways and flush it away down the loo. It is important if you do want to flush it away that it is torn, otherwise you may find it is reluctant to leave the toilet bowl! If you're in public loos it often means just dropping it into the blue box which is usually placed beside the toilet. If there isn't one there, then dispose of it as you would do at home.

Lately, there seems to have been a revolution in sanitary towels as they are much thinner than they used to be and so are less conspicuous but more

absorbent. You will find they are much more
comfortable to wear than the traditional 'mattress'.

TAMPONS – 'MICE'

If you don't fancy 'mattresses' or, for instance, you
want to go swimming, then there are always the
alternative 'mice'. Tampons, as they are known, are
the modern day phenomena which many women
could not live without! They do exactly the same
job but lie inside your body rather than outside.

There is an art to using 'mice' which can take a bit
of practice and getting used to. The key word to
success is relaxation. If you are tense, then your
muscles in the vagina will be too and you will find
you are fighting a losing battle! A good idea is to
lock yourself in the loo with a new box (when you
have got the time) and practice until it feels right.

They come with or without a cardboard or plastic
applicator – a little tube which holds the 'mouse'
and puts it exactly where it should be. Until you
become familiar with your own body then these are
probably the best kind of 'mice' to use. The trouble
with an applicator though, is that it is quite difficult
to flush down the loo – so you often find yourself
having to fish it out and throw it into the bin, or
wait until the toilet cistern refills and have another
go! If you choose 'mice' without applicators, you
won't have this problem and they have the added
advantage of being very easy to disguise in a

21

clenched fist!

Once the 'mouse' is inside you, you should be unaware that anything is there. If you can feel something then it is not in the right position – it is probably not in far enough. Don't worry about pushing it in too far as it will stop itself when it can't go any further – it is practically impossible to lose a mouse. A string hangs outside your body and should be gently pulled when you want to remove the tampon.

If you have to tug hard then the tampon is not ready to come out. As the menstrual blood fills up the tampon, it will get heavier, and will in effect begin to push itself out. Pull the string downwards in the direction of your knees.

Because they do fit so comfortably inside you, it is quite common to forget about them. However it is not recommended that tampons are worn for more than four hours without changing them (although in reality everyone disregards this). It is in your best interest if you do stick to this rule as it could lead to leakages or even infections in extreme circumstances. For this reason they are not very good for night use, unless you are a light sleeper! There will be accidents and your knickers or sheets will be soiled. It is hard to get it right all the time even if you have been menstruating for years. Don't just throw your soiled garments into the dirty linen basket, rinse them in cold water with a bit of soap first otherwise they'll stain.

If you are still unsure about using tampons, there are very good, easy to read and understand instructions on the back or inside all brands. If you still have problems perhaps you could discuss it with your mum or a friend.

WHAT'S RIGHT FOR YOU?

How do you decide if you are a 'super deluxe' or a 'teeny weeny' 'mattress' or 'mouse'? We all feel as if we are losing pints of haemoglobin (blood), when in reality we are told it is only one tablespoon. How do you judge if your tablespoon requires light, regular, medium or heavy protection? In fact, during one period, you will probably need them all! For the first day or two, the flow is likely to be at its heaviest. The last few days are likely to be light and this is when it is best to use 'mattresses', as 'mice' may feel uncomfortable. It is wise to wear something a few days before and after your period in case of any leaks which could occur. You will be able to judge what your regular flow is after a while, but until you know better, go for the safe bet. You tend to lose less blood at night because you are inactive; the longest length of time you will go without changing is at night and once you get up, the blood will rush down, so make sure you take this into account when choosing which absorbency to use, otherwise you will be rushing to the loo in a state of panic.

The 300 to 500 periods in one lifetime can cause a lot of discomfort, trauma and expense. There is actually more VAT (Value Added Tax – extra money which is put on by, and goes directly to, the government) on a packet of sanitary towels or tampons than on a packet of cigarettes! This implies that female hygiene is regarded by those in power as a luxury rather than a necessity. Just think how much pocket money will be spent on those luxurious 300 to 500 periods over the years!

THE PAIN OF IT ALL

Although monthly cycles are usually quite straightforward, most women experience some discomfort and pain. Period pain generally comes in the form of nausea and stomach cramps. It can make you feel uncomfortable, but agonising pain is nor normal. If you are suffering extreme discomfort, then a trip to the doctor is advisable. The most obvious solution to easing pain is to take a tablet. There are a vast array of period pain 'cures' available, many of them homeopathic. If you are at home, put a hot water bottle on your stomach; it can alleviate some pains. Gentle exercise, although probably what you least feel like doing, is also supposed to work wonders.

PMS

A week or two before the big event, many women seem to undergo a Doctor Jekyll/Mister Hyde type of mental transformation, along with some physical discomfort. If you do notice that you suffer from any of the following:

- depression
- outbreaks of spots
- short-temperedness
- irritability
- moodiness
- tearfulness
- hot flushes
- bloated stomach
- sore boobs

then you are probably one of the 75 per cent of women who suffer from PMS (Pre-Menstrual Syndrome). Even if you don't notice any personality change, you might find those around you do, as some females are oblivious to it! It is also interesting to note that over half of female crimes are committed during this time.

By the time you reach mid-life (about 50), you can breathe a sigh of relief as menstruation is almost over. When periods come to an end it is called the 'menopause' – often referred to as 'the change'. It marks the end of baby-making years and many women see it as confirmation that they are getting old. However, it is not over that easily. Your hormones are back in the spotlight once more, and going for one final fling. Boy, do they know how to party!!

Chapter Three

SILKY SKIN

STOP THE DEMISE OF THE DERMIS – GENERAL SKIN CARE

It is extremely important that from an early age you begin to treat your skin with the respect it deserves. It is not just a substance which holds your bones and muscles in place, it is far more complex than that! It consists of two main layers – the epidermis which is the outer skin which you can see and the dermis which is the lower layer underneath the roots of the body hair. In the dermis there are blood vessels, oil glands and a layer of body fat. Skin is a reflection of general health. If you are not healthy, your skin will not look healthy. You must eat properly and feed it with the correct balance of vitamins and nutrients (see Chapter One).

The epidermis varies considerably depending on its whereabouts on the body. Compare the skin on your nose to that on your knee. One is likely to be very dry, the other greasier.

The surface of the skin becomes incredibly dirty during the day. You don't need to work in a coal mine to pick up dirt and grime from the environment. As well as dirt landing on you, you produce it yourself. It is far less obvious but it comes in the form of perspiration and oil production from your glands.

THE DREADED SPOT

Blackheads, whiteheads and spots – they're all formed when the sebaceous gland, which is just below the epidermis, produces too much oil. This clogs up the follicle and produces:

1) A blackhead. If the follicle is open, the trapped oil will be exposed to the air which turns it black. This is when a blackhead is formed. Everyone has blackheads – they are only visible if there is a large amount of oil. When a blackhead becomes infected it turns into a spot, which is often filled with pus.
2) A whitehead is just the same as a blackhead – only it is covered with dead cells. As the air hasn't reached it, it hasn't turned black.

SPOTLESS: HOW TO AVOID SPOTS
Prevention is better than cure, so always keep your face as clean as possible. Use a medicated face wash if you have problem skin.

Captivating Clichés
'Eating chocolate and chips causes spots.'

This is both true and untrue. A hormone called 'androgen' can be blamed for spots. It is always present in varying doses and if there is a lot of it present, then it can stimulate oil production and so lead to spots.

However, if your diet consists of too much sugar and fat, then your skin is bound to suffer as it is not getting the correct balance of vitamins and nutrients. This makes it vulnerable to spots. If you touch your face after you have eaten these foods, the skin can become irritated, thus causing spots.

OUT, OUT DAMN SPOT!

The only way to get rid of a blocked pore (a whitehead or a blackhead) is to remove it. This may sound like fun, but it should be considered a complex operation if it is to be successful.

1) Tie your hair back from your face.
2) Pour hot water into a bowl.
3) Place your head over the bowl and a towel over your head to seal in the steam.
4) Stay there for several minutes to open the pores.
5) Remove your head from the bowl and put clean tissues over your fingertips.
6) Gently press the area around the blocked pore and ease it out. Do not dig in your finger nails. If it

will not budge, do not force it as this may only lead to scarring and irritate it even more.

7) Close the pores quickly by splashing cold water onto the face.

pour hot water into bowl

put head over bowl and seal in moisture

cover fingertips and gently squeeze pore

splash on cold water to close open pores

Ideally, this should be done every week or so to keep a clear complexion and reduce the chances of spots developing from the blocked pore which has been left to fester. Most spots clear up after a week or so by themselves, but if you really can't live with a bulging yellow headed spot, and you are tempted to squeeze it, do it properly. Don't use your fingertips unless they are clean or covered with tissue. Dirty fingers that touch spots will encourage them to spread. Always put a dab of astringent (a lotion which contains chemicals to keep pores free from bacteria) on afterwards.

THE SPOT PLAGUE: ACNE

Acne vulgaris isn't just one spot – it's a whole colony of them which can cover not just your face, but also your shoulders and back. Acne is actually a hereditary disease. It can cause scarring if left unattended. However there are all sorts of cures for it – consult your doctor as the best ones are by prescription only. A doctor will also be able to advise on the best diets for acne.

SKIN TYPES

To reduce the number of spots you get, try to identify your own skin type so you know how best to deal with it. There are a wide range of skin types but they roughly fall into three categories.

OILY
Oily skin is most likely to be prone to spots and blackheads because of the over-active sebaceous glands. Keep the skin as clean as possible, washing it regularly and whenever it begins to feel greasy. Use an astringent afterwards.

DRY
Dry skin feels very tight, especially after washing, and it flakes off easily. It is essential to use a moisturising face wash rather than soap, which is notorious for drying all skin types. Afterwards, apply a good moisturiser liberally.

COMBINATION
Combination skin is the most common. It is skin which is greasy on the forehead, nose and chin (the

'T' zone) and drier on the cheeks. Wash your face with a face wash, attack the oily bits with an astringent and apply a moisturiser.

TO WASH OR NOT TO WASH

Facial skin and skin on the neck should not be treated in the same way as other skin. It needs a lot more care and attention, as it is exposed to the elements. The process of washing your face and neck should not be as straightforward as you may think.

Many of us would not think twice about picking up a bar of highly-scented soap first thing in the morning, lathering away at our faces, rinsing it off

with warm water and rubbing a towel briskly over. If this seems familiar to you, then hopefully by the end of the next few paragraphs you will cringe in horror at the thought!

First of all, you do not need to use soap to get facial skin clean. If you do, use an unscented one, preferably with vitamin E added, which is excellent for the skin. Perfumed soaps dry all skins types out, which leads to problems with wrinkles in later life. Sensitive skins in particular do not react well to them.

Secondly, rinsing with warm water opens up pores. Unless you want them to stay open for some time and invite a selection of dirt to settle, it is advisable to close them again. This can be done quickly and simply by rinsing with cold water. Of course, it will take a little bit of courage, but your skin will feel really fresh and it will most definitely wake you up!

Finally, don't rub your face dry. Your skin needs to be treated as gently as possible as it is continually renewing itself and is extremely delicate. Rubbing a rough towel over it does very little good as it is abrasive and just takes off layers of fine skin. Pat it dry. It might take a bit longer but it will certainly be worth it in the end.

Are you cringing with shame yet? Are you guilty of one or more of the above? Then read on! There are three little golden rules to stick to if you want healthy-looking skin for the rest of your life.

CLEANSE, TONE, MOISTURISE – THREE VITAL STEPS

CLEANSING
Cleansers come as lotions, washes, scrubs and packs and take off the excess dirt from the skin's surface.

face pack

face scrub

face mask

They are usually chosen with a specific skin type or problem in mind. They should be applied liberally and then removed completely. The more 'heavy duty' face cleansers, like mud packs for instance, have a better effect if used only once or twice a week, as a special treat; otherwise your skin will get 'used' to it. These packs have to be left on for several minutes to harden and dry before they are removed, either by peeling them or washing them off.

TONING

Toners remove the finer traces of grime left behind. It is quite amazing to see how dirty a 'clean' face can actually be sometimes. Again, they come in various forms for specific skin types and are usually water-based. They should be applied to cotton wool and swept across the face, giving special attention to the more oily areas where the grime is especially stubborn.

MOISTURISING

Moisturising the skin is very important and even if you ignore every other aspect of skin care, do try to remember this stage. After washing, your skin can dry out very quickly causing it to resemble a raisin if left unattended. You only have to sit in the bath for half an hour and look at your fingertips to see what water can do to your skin. That is why it is important to replace the nutrients you lose. This can be done either by adding bath oil to the water rather than bubble bath (which has a tendency to dry the skin out) which is the equivalent of moisturising as you soak or by applying cream afterwards. Moisturiser will replace the lost skin moisture and so keep it supple and healthy rather than dry and wrinkly.

DON'T LET THE SUN SHINE DOWN ON YOU

It is not only water that can have a drying effect. Another enemy of the skin is the sun. The sun's rays actually age the skin by drying it out.

These days it is fashionable to have a sun tan. This was not always the case. In the last century, tanning was undesirable as it showed you must have been from the lower classes, meaning that you had to work outside for a living. Sunbathing can be quite a dangerous trend. The process appears to be very simple – you lie in the sun and a chemical in your skin called melanin (which decides what skin and hair colour you have naturally) reacts, giving you a tan.

However, pale skins are not meant to be exposed to harmful sunrays, so they can react badly if they are not properly protected. It is imperative that you use protection in the form of suntan lotions. As your skin is young, it won't have had much exposure to the sun's rays, so it would be best to opt for high factor lotions, such as factor 15 or above, for the first few days you spend in the sun. This will enable you to stay in the sun up to 15 times longer than you could without the lotion on, with the same effect. This may well be a shorter length of time than you might have expected as sunshine can be very intense and extremely damaging. Not only do you risk getting burned, which is very painful and from which your skin will take a long time to recuperate, but there is growing evidence of skin cancers developing from over-exposure to the sun, especially if it is intense and the skin is very pale.

If you are going sunbathing, never overdo it. Let your skin get used to the sun slowly. This will give the skin a chance to get accustomed to the new environment and the melanin in it will be able to react. This is preferable to it just burning so you have to spend the rest of the tanning time indoors and in pain. Gradual tanning lasts longer anyway, and is much safer.

After several days on the high factor lotions, you can gradually move down to the lower ones, but be sensible. Remember, if you are going in the water, to apply it before and after your swim and to use a lotion which won't immediately wash off, so it gives you protection while you're in the water. Water magnifies the rays making them even more lethal because you feel cool and do not notice them as much.

Areas to be particularly concerned about are:

- nose
- ears
- breast bone
- hips
- shins
- shoulders

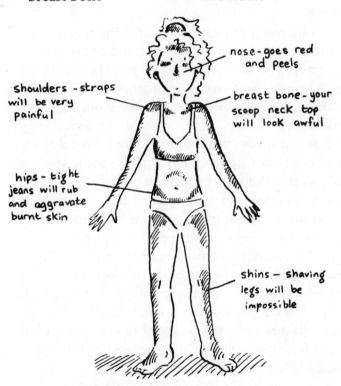

nose - goes red and peels

shoulders - straps will be very painful

breast bone - your scoop neck top will look awful

hips - tight jeans will rub and aggravate burnt skin

shins — shaving legs will be impossible

These are all places where the skin is not very deep and where it is generally stretched across a prominent bone, thus making it especially likely to burn. Use a sunblock on these places if you wish as it will prevent almost all of the sun's rays getting through.

After a hard day's sunbathing, it is vital to remoisturise your skin by using an aftersun. This cools the skin down and gets it ready for the next session.

It is important to use sun creams and moisturisers even if you are just out in the sun and not really sunbathing. It is easy to forget if you are not trying to go brown that you can get burned anyway, by walking, playing tennis and just being outside when it is sunny.

You can always use false tans. They have the same effect and are safer and quicker. Some last only a matter of hours although others can 'dye' the skin making it more permanent. There are hundreds of brands to choose from and they come in a liquid or cream form which you apply with fingers or cotton wool. Always read the instructions well and practise before the big night. Don't forget to consider every possible piece of flesh that will be on show. For temporary tans, a handy tip is to take an umbrella out with you in case of rain. Everyone has heard at least one horror story about streaky legs caused by an unexpected downpour.

Chapter Four

HEAVENLY HAIR

HAIR CARE

No matter what your hair is – long, short, straight
or curly – it has to be looked after to look good.

your hair should suit your face and personality –
not just the latest fashion or style

Healthy looking hair is an asset to every girl and just takes that little bit of extra care and attention. It needs to be cut, cleaned and combed. How much or how little depends on your type of hair.

Captivating Clichés
'Brushing your hair 100 times every night and morning will make it silky and smooth.'
   Many hairdressers say this is nonsense, that what it gives you is split ends and greasier hair and that you should just comb it lightly and run your fingers through it to untangle it. However, other hairdressers believe in brushing vigorously. So the answer really is that it's up to you.

HAIR TYPES

GREASY HAIR
During puberty, you may find you have a particular problem with greasy hair. This can be caused by enthusiastic sebaceous glands again, which means the hair will need frequent washing with a strong shampoo, specially formulated for this specific hair type.

greasy hair

DRY HAIR

This will need less frequent washing with a mild shampoo. There are a number of moisturising conditioners and oil treatments which can help your hair, so shop around for a suitable one for you. Dry hair tends to be prone to split ends and can be fly-away, especially after washing.

split ends

fly away hair

NORMAL HAIR

Very few teenagers have this kind of hair. It should be washed whenever you feel it necessary with a fairly mild shampoo and conditioned afterwards.

43

SHAMPOO – THE DIFFERENCE IT CAN MAKE TO YOUR LIFE

When choosing a shampoo, decide which category your hair falls into and get at least two different brands. Hair actually gets used to a certain product and after a while it will become less effective. If you rotate the two shampoos, your hair will 'stay on its toes' and react well.

HAIR WASH

1) Before washing your hair, put your head upside down and massage it, or brush your hair vigorously. This will rush the blood to your head, and in effect 'feed' the follicles as well as loosening dirt, grime and dandruff.
2) When washing hair, use warm water first to open the pores and cool water to rinse and so close the pores. If the water is too hot then it will activate the grease glands in the head.
3) Put a blob of shampoo into the palm of your hand. The blob should be about the size of a 50 pence piece, but slightly bigger if your hair is long or very thick.
4) Apply it to the scalp when the hair is thoroughly wet and work it in, massaging lightly. This too will stimulate the blood supply in the head and make your hair look healthier.

5) Resist the urge to rub shampoo into the ends. This will only weaken the hair shaft and cause split ends.

6) Rinse your hair well as by doing so it will clean the ends sufficiently. If the shampoo is not removed properly, your hair will look dull and lifeless.

7) If your hair feels really dirty, give it one more wash. Manufacturers often advise this anyway, purely so that you will use more of their product!

How often you wash your hair is entirely up to you. If it is dry, try not to wash it too often. However, if you live in a busy city, you may need to wash it every other day because of the grime in the atmosphere. If so, make sure you use a mild shampoo. Experiment and see what works for you. Generally though, it should be washed at least once a week.

Captivating Clichés
'Rinsing your hair until it squeaks means that it is clean.'

This is more or less true, however it is possible to have clean ends and shampoo-coated roots which is no good at all. The squeak is caused by water cleaning the hair and unless the shampoo has done its job too, you may find the hair will look clean for a very short period of time. Pulling hair to achieve the squeak in the first place is not recommended anyway, as it can do a lot of damage.

HAIR-RAISING HORRORS

SPLIT ENDS

These resemble the branch of a tree, full of little twigs and can be a real problem particularly for people with dry hair. There is only one real solution and that is to have them cut off. A good trim every six weeks or so should keep them at bay. Ignore any advertisement which claims to cure them. However, certain products can do a good job of disguising them by flattening them down, and many can actually strengthen the hair, like conditioners for example. You will be more prone to split ends if you wear your hair tied back a lot or if you brush it when it is wet. Make sure anything you tie around your hair is coated with a protective layer and is not just exposed plastic.

DANDRUFF

Dandruff can occur in any hair type and is caused as particles of dead skin flake off and collect on the scalp and hair roots. It can be treated with special dandruff shampoos which work quite quickly and successfully.

CAREFUL CONDITIONING

The most important step in washing hair comes afterwards in the form of conditioning it. There is a very wide selection of conditioners on the market ranging from frequent use to more intensive treatment such as hot oil or wax. For any to have maximum effect, treatments must be applied to towel dry hair, and left on for the suggested amount of time. The treatments will put lost moisture back into the hair, making it softer and easier to handle. These, too, need to be rinsed off completely. Again, experiment to find which is best for you.

Star Tip
When washing your hair, get into the habit of washing your combs and brushes in warm soapy water. Dirty ones can encourage dandruff and harbour grease and grime. Rinse the soap off well and for brushes, leave them to dry face down on their bristles if possible, so all excess water is removed.

47

GET IT DRY

Use a comb or a hairbrush with widespread prongs and bobbles on the end which protect the hair. Always squeeze excess water, never wring your hair or rub it.

If you do have the time, always let your hair dry naturally. Hair dryers are very convenient but do your hair no favours in the long run. They dry the hair out so will often give it the appearance of fuzziness. If you do need dry hair fast, use the drier on a cold setting. This will do less damage and make it more manageable.

There are a variety of nozzles to attach to the end of the humble hair dryer. Ones which open out are good for an all-over dry, ones which come to a narrow, flat edge are suitable for blow drying specific areas and direct the heat exactly where it needs it, often at the roots to give the hair lift. Bending your head over and fluffing up your hair can also do this. The diffuser is the newest addition. These are very large, circular adaptors with lots of little protrusions. These enable the heat to be evenly distributed and so give maximum volume to your hair and keep curly hair curly. The real advantage is that diffusers aren't frightfully expensive.

HAIR STYLING

MOUSSE, GEL AND HAIRSPRAY

Styling hair can often be made easier by using mousse, gel or hairspray. All of them hold a style in place to some extent. Some should be applied when hair is wet, others after it has been dried.

Mousse should be applied to the roots and worked outwards. It gives body and volume to the hair but still allows it to move naturally. Never put too much on and keep the amount to about the size of a small ball in the palm of your hand (depending on the length and thickness of the hair again), otherwise it will make a sticky mess.

Gel should be applied with the finger tips and worked into the roots, or else just 'slick' it over for a wet look on shorter styles, which it is best suited to. It will give a more 'set' result than mousse.

If your hair is curly, a hair wax or pomade will help control the frizz. Just a bit on the palm of your hand and then rubbed through the hair will do the trick.

Hairspray is not something restricted to mums. It now comes in ozone-friendly spray pumps and is put on as the final touch to your style, and will hold it firmly in place. It may feel rather stiff and uncomfortable afterwards, especially if you put on too much.

Try and use these products sparingly as they do attract dirt and grime so don't just use them because everybody else does. However, if your hair is limp it may benefit from these products. Beautiful, bouncy hair can be a girl's biggest asset.

FEEL THE BURN

Another way of styling hair involves heat, such as tongs, rollers, crimpers or straighteners. All these work by 'burning' the hair into shape. Try not to use any of them too frequently because they are not the best things in the world for your hair to have to endure as you can imagine. Hair cannot repair itself as quickly as the skin can. It has to regrow from the roots which can take a long time. It only grows approximately one centimetre or thereabout every month, though the hopefully-improved weather in summer means it should move faster then!

PRETTY PERMS

Perms provide you with a 'perm'anent style. They
work by breaking down the natural structure of the
hair with chemicals. The hair is then reshaped and
set around curlers. If you want a perm then go to a
professional. Too many disasters occur with home
perming kits for you to take the risk. And because
they are a permanent change to your hair they will
be around until they grow out. You could be stuck
with a long-term disaster! There are lots of perm

types to choose from, light, loose, tight, root,
pincurl – to name but a few. Ask the stylist for a full
description of each one. Remember, perms have to
be well-maintained to stay looking good so think
whether you are prepared for all that extra hassle

and hard work involved before going for it. They can also take a great deal of 'mum persuading' as they can be expensive!

HAIR DYES

Hair dyes have been used for over 3000 years. The ancient kings of Babylon would adorn their locks with gold dust! Hair colour is determined by melanin which is also responsible for skin colour and tanning as previously mentioned. If you decide you are not too keen on the colour nature gave you then you can change the colour. A dye should be used to enhance your own colour, not to produce a brand new one, as dramatic changes usually look very artificial. Brown hair can look good as bronze or chestnut, red hair can go copper or Titian and mousey hair can go honey or gold very successfully.

If you are buying a dye, read the packet carefully. See whether the dye is temporary, semi-permanent or permanent. It might be wise to go for the temporary look so you can see what it is like first. They leave a slight colour deposit on the surface of the hair which is removed gradually after a few washes, so it may be easier to talk Mum into letting you do this.

Semi-permanents last longer as they actually penetrate the surface of the hair shaft. Permanent dyes last until they grow out, which can cause

unsightly roots, so it would probably take a lot of
persuasion on your behalf if you are really sure you
want a complete change. (Never use hair dyes on
eyebrows or eyelashes. If you do want to dye them,
see a professional.)

Natural substances like henna and lemon juice
can be used to change hair colour. Henna is a
greenish powder which mixes into a paste and gives
a red hue to practically any colour hair. It is quite a
messy, smelly process and can last up to two or
three months. A splash of red wine makes it deeper
and lemon juice will speed up the dyeing process.
Lemon juice has been used for centuries to make
hair lighter in the sun and can have practically the
same effect as peroxide. It also strips the hair thus
making it incredibly dry afterwards.

TAKE THAT CUT

A simple hair cut can be one of the most traumatic things you could ever do to your 'crowning glory'.

First of all, decide on a style you fancy. Be realistic though. Just because your desired haircut resembles a mega-star's, it does not mean your face or your figure will. It will still be you, but with a different hairstyle. Bear in mind that your hair may not 'do' the style you wish to have and if it is a very fancy one that needs a lot of looking after and fiddling with in the morning, will you realistically have two hours to waste on it before school?

Think whether you will actually suit the style you decide on. Ask the stylist's advice. Generally speaking, if you have a long face go for short hair, if you have a round face go for longer hair.

Star Tip
Look in magazines for ideas. Keep a selection of cuttings and get a recent photo of yourself of the right size and try superimposing your face over the models' for a very rough and quick visual idea of what you may look like.

Finding a reputable stylist with whom you can bear to put your life in their hands can be a bit tricky. You should not feel obliged to take your custom to Kwik Kutz just because it has been your mum's 'local' for 20 years! However, do not be too

quick to dismiss it either. It may be just as good, or
better, than the latest designer salon. Just because
somewhere has a designer name, decor, uniforms
and model-like employees does not necessarily
mean the standard of work is any better. If you do
feel, though, that you want to escape the threat of a
purple or blue rinse then go in search of somewhere
you feel instinctively comfortable with. Ask for
other people's opinions and remember, prices can
vary considerably so shop around. If you are on a
tight budget, it can be a major drawback.

Star Tip
Many large hairdressing chains have to train students and may be on the lookout for real live guineapigs for them to experiment on. They usually have a very specific thing to practise so do not expect to tell them what you want, but if you are feeling adventurous, then go for it. They are also a lot cheaper than their qualified colleagues.

It is wise though not to settle for the cheapest option. If you know that a salon has an excellent reputation but is rather pricey, then save up for it. Your hairstyle is going to be there for a long time so think of it as an investment.

When you have decided on a stylist, take the magazine cuttings with you. Talk to them about your choices, they can advise you which will look better on you just by considering your face shape. Listen to them to some extent. After all they have spent years in training, but never let them bully you into saying yes to something you really don't want. If you are sure you do want something specific, and they are not too keen on doing it, there may be a real reason for it. If you still insist on it and are not happy with the result, they are likely to be unsympathetic as it will be a case of 'I told you so'. If, on the other hand, you did take their advice and were horrified with the result, stick to your guns and demand that they fix it for you. It is in their interest to keep the customer happy as bad publicity

travels fast. There have even been cases of people taking hairstylists to court over the trauma and subsequent psychological strain the customers have been through!

If you do not want to be disappointed then do not opt for a dramatic change. Going from down-your-back locks to a short crop can be very distressing and practically every woman has at least one 'haircut from hell' horror story to tell. If you do really want a drastic change, then think about doing it gradually. That way you will get used to shorter hair slowly so it will be less of a shock.

Chapter Five

YOUR BEAUTIFUL, BEAUTIFUL BODY

Puberty marks the start of womanhood for girls and is responsible for the quite dramatic changes in your body. You may experience these 'symptoms' all together, separately or in a different order. As everyone is unique there are no set rules you have to follow! Your figure (boobs, waist, hips, legs) is the figure you have inherited from your parents. Most women and girls say that they hate their bodies. Don't fall into that negative trap if you can help it. Learn to like your body. There are certain things you can do to improve it with exercise and a good diet, but essentially you will be one of the shapes outlined here.

Accept what you are, talk to your family and friends about it and think of all the beautiful women in the world and all the various shapes and sizes they are. It would be a very boring place if we were all the same after all.

YOUR SHAPE

You may have noticed that your hips have suddenly started to move outwards. This is because, yet again, the woman's body is getting itself ready for reproduction of the species. The baby will be kept between the hips for nine months and it has to be comfortable with enough space to move around. Your hips have to be wide enough to accommodate a baby if you do decide to have one at some point.

Figures can be a variety of shapes and sizes as we are all individual, but they generally fall into one of these categories:

'PEAR' SHAPED FIGURE

This means it is bottom heavy. You have a delicate build above the waist, your shoulders are narrower than the hips and you have a defined waist.

THE 'HOUR GLASS' FIGURE

This is the envy of most females as it means you have balanced shoulders, bust and hips and a defined waist.

'RECTANGLE' FIGURE

This has straight hips, a flat bottom and little definition of the waist.

'TRIANGLE' FIGURE

This has shoulders which are broader than the hips, a defined waist, straight hips, a narrow pelvis and slim lower legs.

BOOBS

You may also have noticed some strange movement occurring on your chest and realise your vest no longer fits! This is very likely to be because your boobs are growing. They begin life as little lumps just under your nipples. Again this is all part of the preparation for reproduction, this time for feeding the baby.

Meanwhile, it is time to get rid of that vest and

get ready to wear a bra or crop top. This can be a pretty big step and the idea of wearing such uncomfortable contraptions can be rather scary. The reason we wear them is for support. They also stop you bouncing around too much. You may prefer a crop top to a bra, which give less support but tends to be more comfortable and appropriate if your boobs are quite small.

Choosing a bra is not just a case of going into a shop, picking one out, buying it and wearing it. First of all, you have to know what size you are looking for. Get a tape measure, and put it around your body, just under your bust. If the measurement in inches is even then add four to the number; if it is odd add five. (This number will be referred to as x.) Although most things in life these

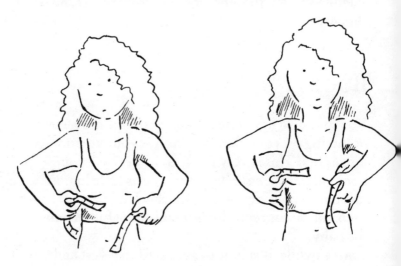

mum, what does 52cm mean?

days are referred to in centimetres, bras are an exception and are generally still measured in inches. You should by now have a number like 32, 34, 36 and so on.

Now you have to find your cup size. In case you have never noticed, boobs come in many shapes and sizes and up till now the only thing you have

what's your cup size?

measured is your back size. Measure your bust across the fullest part. The difference between this (y) and x will determine your cup size. (That is, the letter which will come after the number.)

If the two are the same you will need an A cup, if *y* is one inch bigger than *x* you will need a B cup, if it is two inches bigger then it will be a C cup and so on. These days manufacturers go up to a FF (double F) or a G cup. If you suspect you are any bigger than that you may have difficulty finding a bra! (There is also a AA cup (double A) which is really just a training bra to get you used to wearing one.)

You now have to decide what kind of bra you want. There are padded bras, underwired bras, wonder bras, sports bras, strapless bras and backless bras. The first four are for extra support and the other two are for those more revealing outfits which may otherwise be spoilt. All you need to do then is find your size number, find one you like and buy it. You may find that for the first few days you feel a bit uncomfortable. This is partly because you are not used to wearing something like this in the first place and also because it is new and will take a bit of wearing in like any new article of clothing. After a while you will hardly notice you are wearing one at all. You should check your measurements every few months until you reach the age when you stop growing (somewhere between 18 and 21). Never try to squeeze into a bra you know is too small for you. As well as it being painful on your boobs it will dig into your back and may cause you more problems later on. If you find your bra rides up at the front then it is too big. If it rides up at the back, digs into your shoulders or your boobs then it is too small.

Body Hair

As well as these little protrusions, there may also be some very strange bits of hair sprouting in some unusual places! Hair, if it's anywhere other than on

your head, is yet another of those taboo subjects which no-one really talks about even though every adult has it and every teenager is terrified of it. The reason we all have it stretches back to the days of cave men and women. They were practically covered in fuzz and we have still got some of it covering our vital parts. It was always thickest where our ancestors needed it most, to keep warm or for extra protection. Hair reacts as an insulator by trapping in air and keeping it close to the skin. Our heads, for example, are covered in hair because it is from here that we lose one third of all our body heat. Watch the small hairs on your arm stand up when you shiver. Hair is also there to collect dirt. We have eyebrows and eyelashes to collect dirt and so protect our eyes, and we also have hair under the arms and in the genital region (pubic hair) where there are sweat glands.

TO DE-FUZZ OR NOT TO DE-FUZZ?

Many European women are not bothered in the least by their fuzziness, and think it is attractive and feminine. However, most British women think it looks unsightly and harbours dirt so remove it. Underarm and leg hair are usually the first to go, and a lot of women remove it from their bikini line too. It is quite common for pubic hair to extend to the top of the legs, which can ruin nice underwear or sports outfits (according to British women anyway!).

Captivating Clichés
'Once you remove hair, it will grow back twice as quick and twice as thick.'
    Actually, this one does appear to be true, but in fact isn't. Body hair grows to a certain length, then it

stops. It has a tapered end and as soon as this is cut off, it will grow back more bluntly, thus feeling more coarse.

This then gives the impression of thickness. As the hair knows it is supposed to be a certain length, it does you the favour of growing back!

DEFOLIATION

There are several ways of de-fuzzing bits, some are easier and less painful than others:

1) Shaving is the most common defuzzing method, and also one of the quickest. It can be done on wet skin with a conventional razor or dry skin with an electric one (although some razors have now been developed that can be used on either wet or dry skin.

2) Substances called 'depilatories' come in a cream form which were once incredibly smelly but are now much more pleasant and bearable. They remove the hair by dissolving it right down to the root. You leave it on the hairy area for a few minutes and then remove it thoroughly with water. Sometimes, depilatories react with sensitive skins so it is always wise to do a patch test on a small area first.

3) Waxing can be done either professionally, or at home after a lot of practice. Wax on strips is now the more convenient kind as it is less messy than applying it from a tub with a brush. It is placed on the area when the hair is about half a centimetre

long and quickly whipped off in the direction of growth. It actually removes hair from the root, making it weaker when it grows back which is usually quite slow, as the root has to recover! It can be pretty painful so it is worth practising on the legs for example, to master the technique, before trying more delicate areas, such as underarms.

4) Epilators are the newcomers to defoliation techniques. They are hand-held electrical devices which act like tweezers on a large scale. They pull the hair from the root and, like waxing, can be uncomfortable. Both leave the skin very sensitive for at least a few hours afterwards.

5) There is no permanent solution to fuzziness, but the closest thing you will get to it is electrolysis. This is a very expensive and time-consuming process which involves putting a small electrical charge into the root of each hair, which will in effect weaken it and prevent growth for long periods of time, sometimes forever, depending on the strength of the hair.

ARE YOU GLOWING OR SWEATING?

You may also have noticed some unusual smells wafting from your body. Sweat glands begin to get active too and you will suddenly find you have a warm sticky sensation under your armpits after an energetic games lesson. It is particularly important

that you keep yourself clean daily otherwise these smells will begin to linger and get stronger. Don't forget to wash your vagina too, especially when you have got your period. The pubic area has got its own built in cleaning system, but it is not advisable to wait for it to start working. (Remember, when using soap to avoid highly scented ones as they can upset the natural balance of enzymes which can lead to vaginal infections in certain cases.)

Once you are clean all over, don't forget to use a deodorant or antiperspirant under your arms. Never use this near the pubic area or it will have the same reaction as scented soap. Deodorants come either as sprays or 'roll-ons'. They are perfumed and keep the smell of sweat at bay. Antiperspirants which can also come as blocks actually reduce the amount of sweat produced and are sometimes perfumed too. It is dangerous to block up pores completely as the body would then have no way of cooling down, so do not expect to be totally dry for hours on end. Always remember too to wash under your arms to clear the pores of these products before going to bed.

Perfumes can be used to mask odours. They should not be used in this way really – they should be used to give a fresh and pleasant smell. Don't go overboard with perfume and try not to have too many aromas clashing with each other. Perfumes come in sprays, oils or even creams. 'Eau de toilette' is a cheaper alternative to pure perfume or perfumed oil as it is slightly weaker. Pure perfume, like perfumed oils are highly concentrated, which means they will stay on for longer. Be careful of very cheap perfumes, as they are likely to smell pretty nasty when they are on. Always avoid getting perfume on clothes as they stain easily and are bad for materials.

For That Million Pound Smile And The Sweetest Breath In The World

Odours can come from many places in the body! Apart from those mentioned already, another area which needs a lot of attention is the mouth. Bad

breath is something many teenagers suffer from, and in a few circumstances can be blamed on hormones yet again. Generally though, it is down to neglect.

Teeth need to be brushed thoroughly after every meal or debris will collect on them and produce nasty smells as well as causing decay which won't be very nice. Make sure that as well as using a toothbrush (changed every month or so) and paste, you use dental floss too. A brush will clean the flat surfaces but it is in the nooks and crannies between the teeth where the food waste sits happily, causing bad breath and decay. Your second teeth gradually become stronger, but initially they are quite weak. More people have fillings as teenagers than in later life. Therefore, as a teenager, you should be especially careful with your oral care.

If people still turn green when you open your mouth, then perhaps you could change your diet. Garlic, onion and strong tasting foods linger for days. You may find, too, that if you are hungry it will make it worse. Try using a mouthwash after brushing, which can kill some of the smells for a few hours. In exceptional cases, bad breath may be the symptom of physical illness. If you try all the above and your breath still smells, it might be worth a visit to the dentist. (You should, in any case, be going to the dentist every six months. Dentists can give advice on halitosis and nip any problem in the bud. And they're *free* – if you're under 16.)

Star Tip
If you have had garlic or onions, eat some fresh parsley. The chlorophyll in it will take away any nasty, lingering odours.

Many adolescents find they have problems with their second teeth. They might stick out, be uneven or grow in different directions, so a dentist may suggest a brace or plate. This is not the end of the world, although there is no denying it will feel strange and uncomfortable. You may even think it looks terrible, but surely it is better to suffer for a short amount of time rather than for the rest of your life. You really will be amazed at the transformation when it is removed and you are guaranteed to look a lot better afterwards.

TERRIFIC TALONS

Like teeth, nails are made of calcium and face a lot
of daily wear and tear. They can pick up a lot of dirt
and germs during the day, so if you bite them, it is a
far from healthy habit. Apart from that, bitten nails
also look very unattractive. There are plenty of
nail-biting cures to choose from which consist of
painting your nails with a disgusting tasting fluid,
but many only work for a short period of time as
the biter in question gets used to the bad taste. The
only way you can really stop is by deciding you
want to, and having the will-power to stick to it.

Nails enjoy the sunlight and will grow quicker
and stronger if exposed to it regularly. Once they
have grown, you will need to take a lot of care of
them to keep them looking in top shape. It is best to
keep them all at a realistic length. Long nails can
look good, but once one snaps, the rest may as well
follow suit. Rather than cutting them, get into the
habit of filing instead. Don't use a metal file as they
are far too harsh. Always file in the same direction,
never backwards and forwards, as this will weaken
the nail.

If you decide that you want to paint your nails,
make sure your cuticles (the skin at the bottom) are
gently pushed back otherwise they will look untidy.
It is easier to do this when the skin is soft, possibly
after soaking your hands in warm water for a few
minutes. Always apply a clear base coat to nails, or

you may find after removing the varnish that they have become discoloured. Cheaper varnishes chip very easily, so rather than buying several different shades, invest in one good, versatile one. Do not leave varnish on for too long, or the nails will be starved of air and become weak and brittle.

Chapter Six

THE SECRET WORLD OF MAKE-UP

Make-up has been around for thousands of years and there is evidence to suggest it was worn in the earliest civilisations. The reason for women (and men during fashionable periods in history) wearing make-up is to enhance their physical looks and in so doing, make them more attractive to the opposite sex. In fact, make-up imitates certain sexual signs which are emitted when you are 'turned on'. When you are aroused, pupils in the eye get bigger, causing them to look darker, cheeks flush and lips get redder and fuller. When you think about that, eye make-up, blusher and lipstick will never feel the same again!

Generally, parents are reluctant for their daughters to start wearing make-up. If you really want to wear it, try to coax them into letting you, but if they are adamant, don't push too hard. Remember, you will never have such fresh skin (ignoring spots) as you do now. Once you start wearing make-up you will probably never stop using it as you will feel naked without it. Try not to be over-eager to rush into the habit.

If your mother does agree to it, ask her if you can experiment with her old make-up. Talk to her about it, as she may have some handy tips and is bound to be honest in telling you what you look like! This way you will get used to putting it on before you spend any pocket money on it. You could do this with a group of friends. It will be much more fun swapping ideas and comments together rather than being on your own. If they can bring their mums' old make-up with them too there will be a greater variety to try out.

For the beginner who wishes to make their first non-disastrous attempt, here's a quick guide to various products.

A FIRM FOUNDATION

This should be the basis of all your 'work'. It is also one of the most difficult forms of make-up to get right! It is put on all over the face and neck to even out the skin tone, which is usually blotchy. Unfortunately it is probably the hardest purchase to find if you are dark skinned and you may have to try specialist shops. Foundation can come in a variety of containers – bottles, tubs, tubes and jars but they generally take the form of a cream or liquid.

Standing in front of the foundation counter can be quite a daunting experience, so always take a friend along for moral support. A friend also comes in handy for giving an opinion on something, so it is wise to choose one who you know will be honest with you – and not afraid of telling you the truth. If you can't find a friend to go with you, then make use of the shop assistants. They do generally know what they are talking about, but never let them pressurise you into a sale.

Captivating Clichés
'Always test a foundation on the back of your hand for a good match.'

In fact, although this sounds like a reasonable suggestion, it is actually a total waste of time! The skin on the back of your hand is completely different to that on your face, both in texture and tone. Facial skin is exposed to the elements constantly. Think how often your nose gets sunburned, your lips chap in the cold or your freckles come out when it's a nice day. Then consider how often you wear a glove over your head, break out in a bout of acne on your fingertips or blush on the palms when you catch the eye of the hunkiest boy alive!

BUYING YOUR FOUNDATION

The first step is to decide if you prefer the idea of a cream or a liquid. Look at the consistency. See how easy it is to apply (now you can use the back of your hand!).

Generally, cream needs a lot of 'working in' compared to liquids which are just swept quickly across the skin, and is really the easier of the two for beginners.

Use a tester – there are usually hygenic seals preventing you from opening new products – or ask an assistant for advice.

1) Put a small dab onto your face, somewhere around your cheek or forehead and blend it in. It should sit on the surface of your skin and look as if there is nothing there! If you like the way your choice absorbs then you may have found the right brand for you. If not, choose a different brand. Never rush into a purchase – it will almost certainly be a waste of money!

2) If, when it is applied, it looks like a dirty mark or a bruise, then it seems likely that your choice has been incorrect and that the shade you have chosen is too dark. Unless you have been through this process before, expect to go home looking like you have been in a boxing ring!

Try again, on a different part of the cheek or forehead. Once you have got it wrong a few times, you should know when you come across the right one provided you haven't run out of face first!

3) Look at the different shades before you. Always take into account the lighting in the shop. Very often it gives an artificial glow to your skin. Don't be afraid to put some on your face, take a mirror outside and look. It is important to see what it is like in natural light.

4) Now and only now look at the price and the name label. Never make it your top priority to choose a cheap brand unless you know it is good

but don't assume that a brand is good just because it is expensive. Top of the range goods are very expensive and they can put a big hole in a tight budget. However, these should be regarded as investments and are often worth it in the long run. If you settle for a cheaper imitation, that is exactly what you will get and it may cost you twice as much in the end. Never feel obliged though to buy anything if you can't afford it or don't really want it, even if the assistant has been plugging it for twenty minutes! Just say you need some time to think about it!

Star Tip
If you suffer from what is commonly known as 'high colouring', that is rosy cheeks, then there is a foundation you can buy which could save your life. Strangely enough, it is bright green. However, it blends in to a neutral shade when put on the skin but counteracts the embarrassing redness. If you have sallow skin, give it a lift with a lilac tinted foundation which, once again, doesn't stay that colour when applied.

APPLYING YOUR FOUNDATION

When it comes to applying your purchase at home, the urge to put a blob on your finger and rub it in vigorously should be resisted. Foundation should become like a second skin not a thick layer – just a film across it. Never use it as a Polyfiller for covering spots. The way to cover these is dealt with later.

Invest in a decent make-up sponge. It should be used damp, not wet, and helps spread the foundation easily, quickly and evenly. Avoid using fingertips on any part of the face as they are very greasy and incredibly dirty.

1) You need a neat and tidy surface to work on, so always tie your hair back off your face before you cleanse, tone and moisturise. Don't forget to include your neck.

2) Putting blobs in positions around your face can lead to an excess of foundation being present. Take your make-up sponge, dampen it and put a small blob directly onto that.

3) Sweep the sponge across the face and neck, including lips and eyelids. It is important that you include your neck, otherwise you will look as though you are wearing a mask.

CRAFTY CONCEALERS

Blemishes and spots will usually disappear by the time the foundation is on. However, if you are still paranoid about the mini Mount Everest which has developed from nowhere and the black rings under your eyes from a hard night's homework stint, then a concealer is just what you need.

They come in a stick form and should be used sparingly. Do not, however tempting it might be, cake it on a spot otherwise you can be sure it will look worse. Although it can be used straight from the stick a small make-up brush with a sponge tip is ideal. Remember to avoid using fingers! Choose a concealer which is a shade slightly lighter than your skin tone for the best results.

PERFECT POWDERS

These fix the work you have done so far and give it a matt finish. Very often, foundations automatically have powder added so there is no need for a separate one. If you do not use one then your face may look shiny or even greasy afterwards.

Often, powders come with their own sponge which can be used, but a large make-up brush is preferable. This can pick up fine particles and distribute them lightly and evenly over the skin. Powder (or foundation) can be used to give optical illusions. It can define or disguise features you are pleased or uncomfortable about. For example, a double chin can be made to look less obvious by applying a darker shade under the jaw line and a lighter one on the chin bone itself. A wide nose can be thinned out by putting darker strips on either side and a light one on the bone. A round face can be thinned by putting dark strips down the sides of the face and forehead and a lighter one in the middle. Experiment for yourself!

BLOOMING BLUSHER

Blusher – or rouge – comes in a variety of forms – as cream, powder and even as tiny coloured balls in a jar! Cream blushers last longer than any other kind but are hard to handle and can be quite messy. Powder and coloured balls are put on by a large brush. Blusher can be flattering on a face which does not appear to have much obvious bone structure to it, but only when it is applied well. It should not go on in little circles like a clown. Before attempting to apply it to your, so far perfect, made-up face, suck in your cheeks and try to see where your cheek bones really are. They do not run from your hairline to the corners of your mouth, but from your hairline to your nose. It is on that bone that the colour has to go.

Choosing colours is not as straightforward as you may think. It is a good idea to choose pinky browns which will go with practically anything. Do not choose something too dark, keep it to a minimum on the brush and always make it subtle. Remember, you are just enhancing what you have got, not changing your entire bone structure by packing powder on.

1) Keep all your hair off your face
2) Put a small amount of colour on your brush. Place it on the bone near to your hairline and carefully sweep it round, tapering off at the end (just under your eye).

Star Tip
If you wish to emphasise them even more, get a lighter shade – almsot white in fact – and put it above the strip of colour and then put a darker shade on underneath. Remember always to blend it in well and right up the cheek, practically into the hairline.

ELEGANT EYE MAKE-UP

Eyes are the windows to the soul, or so they say, and they are without a doubt extremely important features to any face. Just think how often you look into someone's eyes when you are talking to them or avoid them when you are shy, nervous or lying! We can read an awful lot from someone's eyes – even the state of their health if you are an iridologist! It is very important therefore, that any eye make-up you might wear really emphasises them and brings people's attention to them rather than making them dreary and unattractive.

you don't need to be an Iridologist so see I'm ill

There is an incredibly big selection of products to use for the eyes – eye shadow, eye liner, eye pencil, mascara, but before you consider any, think of the eyebrows.

EYEBROWS
These days, plucking brows to pencil-line thinness is thankfully a thing of the past! However, there probably isn't an eyebrow alive that couldn't do with some tidying up!

Star Tip
Use an old mascara brush if you haven't got an eyebrow brush, dampen it and sweep it across your brows in the direction they grow, to train them.

If after they have been brushed you can see some straggly ones then it is time to get out the tweezers. Never try to remodel your brow shape as you'll only end up ruining it completely – and it will take an awful long time to grow back! The intention is to make the most of what you have got naturally.

Stragglies should only be plucked from underneath brows, never from those on top and the secret is to pull them swiftly in the direction they are growing, not the direction you think they should be growing! The ones near the bridge of your nose are likely to be the ones to bring tears to your eyes. It is better to pluck brows several times a week than saving it all for a once-a-week blitz.

Always give the pores a chance to close before plastering make-up over them. It is wise to pluck your eyebrows at least a couple of hours before you start to get ready.

If you have pale eyebrows which are practically invisible at the best of times, you may find that they disappear completely when you put any make-up on. It is recommended then that you use an eyebrow pencil to go over them and so make them more prominent. Just go over the hairs lightly with a shade close to that of their natural colour. You are not colouring them in, just emphasising them.

EYE SHADOW

Practice with this as much as possible as choosing the right combination of colours is crucial. If in doubt, stick to browns. They will go with almost any hair colour, eye colour or skin tone.

In general:

- Red hair . . . brown, green, gold, coral colours and light shades.
- Blonde and mousy hair . . . brown, coral colours with a pinky tone, light grey and light shades generally.
- Dark hair . . . browns, greys, purples and darker shades.

Star Tip
Before applying any shadow, place a clean hanky under your eye to catch any falling particles of colour which would otherwise destroy all the hard work so far. Also, make sure there is a light film of foundation over your lids as this will enable the colour to stay firmly in place and it will not wear off as quickly.

Choose a small make-up brush or a sponge applicator you feel comfortable with. You could even use a small paint brush with fine, soft bristles.

1) Put the lighter shades on first or you will find that every colour you put on your brush becomes a dirty brown. Always keep another hanky nearby to clean the brush on after each application of colour.

2) Apply a darker shade in the socket line for a deep-set eye look or light ones for a wide-eyed look. Darker colours will make your eyes look smaller, but can also give a more dramatic effect. A lighter colour under the eyebrow will make the eyes look wider.

Remember, both eyes should look the same at the end so do each stage simultaneously otherwise you may forget which colour you used where. Until you have had plenty of practice, the best results will be achieved by keeping the colours simple and subtle – and by blending them well.

If you go to a disco and are wearing eyeshadow, check your eyes in the loo every so often. In the heat shadow melts and there is nothing worse than a

line of colour caught in the crease of your eye as it
melts off your eyelid.

EYE LINER

Eyeliner comes in two forms, as a pencil or as a
liquid. Liquid eyeliner is the newly revived 1960s

fashion statement and it takes a steady hand indeed
to put it on, as well as plenty of practice compared

to the conventional pencil. However, liquid does
seem to last longer; it does not smudge as easily and

gives a very defined look that runs brilliantly in the
rain!

By using an eyeliner, you enclose the eye, giving
the illusion of it being smaller. If your eyes are
already small, stick to light colours and apply them
under the eyelashes on the bottom. If you put any
on the top lid, your eyes will look even smaller.
Putting liner inside the eyelashes encloses the eye
and emphasises the small size.

Keep the colour of the pencil/liquid close to that
of the mascara and remember that very few people –
except those with jet black hair, can get away with
black eye make-up. Brown will always look just
that little warmer and less severe and is far less
likely to give that panda eye effect later on.

MASCARA

It is very important to put this on after your
powder because powder particles will dull the effect
it has.

Star Tip
If your eyelashes are not particularly long or thick, give them a light dusting of face powder or talc before applying your mascara. This will make them look much more impressive!

Many people have the urge to go wild with mascara and put it frantically all over top and bottom lashes which gives a spider-like effect. If that is what you want, then fine, but if you just put mascara on the top and brush it across the bottom very lightly it will look much more natural and flattering.

1) Start with the top lash. Place the brush on top of the eyelashes, nearest to the eyelid and sweep outwards, in one stroke if possible.
2) Put the second coat underneath the lashes and repeat the action.
3) Before you close your eyes, put a hanky underneath your newly made-up lashes and blink onto it a few times. Now you can do the same with the bottom eyelashes.

This will save your foundation from becoming marked.

Captivating Clichés
'When you are using mascara, put the brush in the bottle and pull it out and push it in vigorously to coat it well.'

In actual fact, the best way to coat the brush is to curl it clockwise in the bottle. Look at the bristles on it – they spiral around so have a better chance of picking up mascara filaments that way.

LUSCIOUS LIPS

This should be the final touch to your make-up. Foundation swept over the lips earlier will help fix any colour you put on. Most people apply it straight from the stick, but you will have much better control if you use a lip brush. Many shops sell ones which look rather like paint brushes and come to a point. These are really quite difficult to handle so a flat-edged brush would be better to start off with. Another necessity is a lipliner. Choose one which can be used with several shades of lipstick. If you want a really dramatic effect, use a darker one; this will make your lips look as if they're painted on. A more natural look can be achieved by using a lighter shade than the lipstick itself.

Lipliner is used for two reasons. Firstly, so you know exactly where the lipstick is to go and secondly to prevent the colour bleeding – otherwise you might have a marvellous Coco the Clown effect. (This happens with red colours in particular.)

When using the liner, keep to your natural lip line. If you have thick lips then draw just inside and if they are thin then just outside. Don't be too

91

enthusiastic and don't try to make a completely new shape. Once again, you are just enhancing what you have got.

When choosing colours take into consideration what hair colour, skin tone and lip shape you have! Hair colour is easy -

- Red hair . . . corals, browns, some oranges
- Blonde and mousy hair . . . pinks, corals, no strong shades
- Dark hair . . . deep reds, browns, most strong colours can also be worn

Then consider your skin tone. If it is light then stick to light colours, if dark choose the opposite. And last of all, consider your lip size. If your lips are small, avoid dark shades which will make them look even smaller.

Think about your teeth too. If they are not the whitest of whites then it is not really advisable to wear oranges or corals which will emphasise the fact. To give the impression they are whiter than they really are, stick with plums and reds with a slightly blue tone to them. If you follow all these rules you'll probably only have one colour left! Really, though, if you just wear the colour you feel comfortable in, then you will probably look fine.

When applying it, put one coat on the brush and carefully fill inside the outline you have already drawn on. Blot the first coat and then reapply another. If you want it to last you can buy a lipcoat which holds the colour in place even longer.

Star Tip
If your top lip is larger than the bottom, put a darker shade on it. If the bottom is thicker, put a darker shade here. If they lack that 'puckered up' effect then put a lighter shade in the middle for a fuller lip look!

large top lip

large bottom lip

'puckered up' effect

Golden Rules To Successful Make-Up

- Practice makes perfect. Never attempt a new technique minutes before a big event.
- Have a wide variety of clean brushes and lots of tissues close at hand. Keep brushes clean by washing frequently in warm soapy water a few days before you will need them again as they take a while to dry out thoroughly.)
- If you don't have a favourite colour, don't be afraid of mixing what you do have and experimenting!
- Always blend well and keep it subtle for better effects.
- Always remove make-up thoroughly and never sleep in it! Apart from it looking hideous, it does your skin no favours whatsoever!

Chapter Seven

SENSE YOUR SIZZLING STYLE – CLOTHES

The basic rule is only to wear what you feel comfortable in. Fashions come and go so quickly that it is hard and very expensive to stay up to date all the time. Try not always to buy the 'in' things as they can look dated by the time you have got them home and taken them out of the bag! Go for clothes which won't date immediately and will mix and match with things you have already got. That way you will have a variety of outfits.

Also remember that although fashion changes frequently, your body doesn't. Stuffing yourself into lycra won't look too good if you have got a massive bum or legs like tree trunks. Very long skirts on short people can look silly too. Try to wear something that enhances your appearance whether it is the height of fashion or not!

Star Tip
A 'little black' dress is a really useful thing to have in your wardrobe. It may look pretty simple and

harmless, to the untrained eye of course, but it can be very easily transformed for many different occasions. For a casual look, just throw a jacket over it, glam it up for the evening with jewellery, tights and a belt or even wear it for more formal occasions as it can look elegant, smart and chic. Another vital item is a pair of leggings. Once again, they are highly versatile and can take on a new identity every time you wear them. They are also fairly cheap too.

DON'T SHOP ALONE

When you go shopping, try to take someone with you for help and advice who will give their opinion when you need it. This friend could even be your mum. Many mums have the uncanny knack of telling the truth just when you don't want to hear it!

Do they do refunds at that shop?

It's a bit short!

Is this a fancy dress party?

Spots really show off your acne!

That'd really suit your Cousin Beryl!

Didn't they have your size in it?

Isn't black supposed to be figure flattering?

You did keep the receipt didn't you?

Phrases like 'You're not really going to wear that?', 'Isn't it a bit short?', 'It doesn't do much for your figure', and 'Spots really don't flatter your acne', aren't exactly confidence-inspiring. You might end up buying a garment anyway, just to spite her, but unless your mum really does have a vindictive streak then she is probably only stating the obvious.

However, Mums usually have a very different idea of 'style' to you, and so might dislike anything that you do like, so it's best to go with someone who has similar tastes to your own.

Star Tip
There are a few simple checks you can make to save time trying things on. If the item is black it will make you look thinner, white will have the opposite effect. They will also both set off brilliant white skin perfectly, which does not always achieve the desired look. Stripes of the horizontal kind (left to right) give the illusion of wideness, whereas vertical ones (top to bottom) make you look thinner and taller. Small people who wear long skirts will look smaller, but short skirts will make them look taller. Don't be afraid to try on different clothing and colours to those you are used to wearing. You might find something which looks really good which you may have otherwise disregarded as not 'being you'.

MATERIAL GIRL

There is a wide variety of materials to choose from too. Some cling to bumps and lumps, like lycra for example, others don't. Generally speaking, natural materials are the most comfortable to wear. Cotton is a very cool, natural material that will usually wear well and have a fairly long life if treated properly. Denim is cotton based, but is much more hard-wearing and never seems to go out of fashion. Wool is often mixed with man-made fibres and is cheaper than pure lamb's wool. Silk is a real treat, like satin. However, they can both be mixed with man-made

98

fibres too so again, read the label well. So-called 'man-made' fibres, like polyester, nylon and lycra, are found everywhere. Lycra is most definitely the fashion statement of the 90s. It can be found in one form or another in the majority of shops, but does not necessarily suit everyone. Although its clingy, holding-in properties are good, it is not a miracle worker! Black lycra catsuits do not make everyone appear to have a perfect, sylph-like figure unless they have one in the first place!

It's a good idea to check the washing instructions too. Think carefully before buying something which needs to be hand-washed or dry-cleaned – it is much easier if you can just bung it in the machine.

By now you have chosen the item you fancy buying. Has it been well made? Look at the seams and the stitching and if you are feeling brave give it a little tug. If it comes apart in your hands then you know not to buy it!

Look around as you should find that different shops sell the same or similar things, some of which are more expensive. It may be worth spending the extra pennies if the garment appears to be of a higher quality than the cheaper version as you will probably get more wear out of it. On the other hand, if you get bored with clothes quickly, it might be a good idea to buy the cheaper version, so its life will match your interest in it.

YOUR SIZE

You probably have a rough idea of your size before the shopping expedition but it takes only a few minutes and a tape measure to work it out properly. Put the tape around the fullest part of your bust, your waist and your hips. If your bust is 32 (inches once again), waist 24 and hips 34 then you are a size 10; bust 34, waist 26, hips 36, then you are a size 12 and so on. (You can often buy imported clothes here. Remember that Continental sizes are measured in centimetres and American sizes are one size smaller than ours, for example, an American size 8 is an English size 10.) Of course, you'll probably find that you're top or bottom heavy. While your chest is size 14, your bum is size 8, for instance. Don't worry. Very few people are an *exact* size – your size is the one which your measurements are closest to.

Try finding your size on the rail. If you are under size 10 or over size 12 this can sometimes be difficult. As 47 per cent of the female population are a size 14 or over, then those sizes may possibly have all been sold! Manufacturers very often only cater for Ms Average, the perfect size 10. Your size will probably vary from garment to garment anyway as

some clothes houses are more lenient with their material than others!

Take two sizes into the dressing room. As sizes do vary, it will save time if you do rather than getting changed again and going back out to the rail. If you are only allowed one garment, give the other to your friend to take in.

You must always try something on, even if the idea of entering a communal dressing room makes you break out in a cold sweat. Remember, clothes never look the same on the hanger as they do on you! How come every girl with supermodel looks strips off at the exact moment you enter the changing room?

Often people insist that they are a specific size and then find that the item is too small. If this is the case, don't try to squeeze into something just to save face. Get the next size up and try that instead. Buy the one that you do fit into, not the one you think you should fit into.

When you're going shopping you should always make sure you have got a neat bra and knickers on. It is even more embarrassing going into a communal dressing room if your underwear is in shreds!

Star Tip
Check the colour of the materials in broad daylight as artificial shop lights can give a false impression. Don't forget to tell an assistant what you are doing if it means taking the item in the direction of the door!

Quite a lot of clothes are now electronically tagged and you might find yourself setting off an alarm and getting into an embarrassing situation with a security guard!

If you are trying to match one item with another, make sure that you take that with you when you are shopping so that you can look at the two together.

It is very difficult to remember an exact colour.

If you have tried it on and made sure it fits well, then feeling comfortable in it should come naturally. You are then bound to look good in it, unless of course you have chosen something particularly hideous! (And that is exactly why you need someone with similar taste to yours, to tell you if what you have chosen is horrible or not!) Often we can be blind to what we really look like in something because we have seen what the model advertising it looks like. However, if you absolutely adore something, you should buy it even if your friend hates it. Try to develop style that reflects your own personality and not someone else's. If you do find this difficult to do with the limited selection on offer in most shops, why not try second-hand shops?

SECOND-HAND ROSE

There are usually plenty of them around and they often have a pretty wide selection in them. The clothes there may be old, but they have definitely got character and there is little chance of bumping into someone wearing the same outfit on a Saturday night! Some people just don't fancy the idea, so if you are one of those people then it is obviously not the choice for you. Second-hand clothes should not have any strong odours about them (but they may be a bit musty). If they have any marks or obvious stains on them then don't buy them. You can wash them but the marks have probably been there for a while and are unlikely ever to come off as they will be well absorbed into the fibres. In good shops, clothes are usually washed before they are put on sale, but it's better to be on the safe side and give it another one before wearing it. These clothes may not be in their prime or last very long, but they have definitely got the potential to be unique if you personalise them for yourself and you can pick up some real bargains.

WEEDING YOUR WARDROBE

A good thing to do every few months is to take a look at the contents of your wardrobe. Are you ever going to wear those jeans again or do you really imagine that if they do come back into fashion you will actually be able to fit into them anyway? Be honest with yourself and get rid of them. Don't actually throw them out unless they really have seen better days. They can always be recycled and taken to a second-hand shop where you should get some money for them, or give them to someone you think might want them, such as a little sister or a charity shop.

If you are offered hand-me-downs, don't automatically dismiss them and throw them away.

Look at them carefully. You never know, you might see potential in them.

You can sometimes make old clothes fashionable just with a bit of sewing! You can have a go yourself or take it to a dressmaker, if it really has some potential. If you're learning needlework at school, try to absorb some of the basics as you'll be surprised what you can do and how much money you'll save! For instance, just changing a few buttons or taking a hem up can work wonders!

FOR THOSE FLAT FEET – SHOES

There are so many styles to choose from in the shops that you may not know where to start. If you have limited funds and need a pair that will go with most of your wardrobe, go for a black or brown shoe. They are versatile and can be worn with practically any colour outfit. More specific shades that are chosen with one piece of clothing in mind will probably only go with that piece.

Star Tip
After a hard day's shopping, your feet will be hot and therefore slightly bigger than usual. Bear this in mind. If shoes feel tight then they could get worse after a long night's dancing at the disco, or go sloppy if you are inactive. If you know that you will be wearing the shoes a lot and walking around in them,

106

then do make sure they are comfortable. You don't want to spend too much time 'breaking them in' as it will probably take months as you wait for blisters to heal before getting another pair.

Leather shoes are the kindest on the feet. They let them breathe, so if you are prone to smelly feet then they are especially good. They are also very hard wearing although usually more expensive than man-made varieties. If your parents will let you and you are thinking of taking the plunge and going for a heel, be sensible and realistic in your choice. Can you really see yourself running for a bus in them and would you be allowed to wear them in school?

If you want to wear high heels always start with a small heel first of all, even if you long to look like a rock star in spiky ones. It's better to get used to them gradually rather than make a fool of yourself by tripping up on enormous ones. Remember too, that high heels tend to squeeze toes more than flat shoes and they are incredibly bad for posture and for your back.

AMAZING ACCESSORIES

Like shoes, certain other accessories, such as jewellery, scarves and hair decorations can transform outfits. Don't go too wild with them, as being over decorative can look too busy. If possible, stick to a specific colour so it will give some uniformity to the whole thing. It's best if you just have one important accessory at a time. For example, if you are wearing long earrings then you don't need a necklace and bracelet, and if you are wearing a neckscarf then you don't need a scarf in your hair too.

Although there is quite a wide selection of clip-on earrings available, you'll probably want to have your ears pierced (you might have already had them pierced, of course). It's a good idea to check with your parents before having them done, and always go somewhere reputable. Most places now use stud guns which are both hygienic and quick. These guns fire a stud into your earlobe. They don't hurt, but your ears might sting a bit. If you have sensitive skin, you might find you have to use silver or gold earrings which won't cause a reaction. *Never, ever* pierce your ears yourself.

Chapter Eight

SHRINKING VIOLETS – THE KILLER SHYNESS

Puberty is a very difficult time as you are developing both physically and emotionally. It can be pretty easy to lose touch of who you are and where you are going. Because you are a bit unsure of what is happening to you, you are naturally unsure of yourself. By now, as you are coming to the end of this book, you should at least feel comfortable with your looks or at least more confident about how to make the most of them. Very often feeling good about how you look on the outside makes you feel better about everything else.

Have you ever been in situations where you have experienced the following?

- flushed cheeks, neck and chest
- violently beating heart
- stammering
- inability to string a sentence together – or even speak at all
- difficulty breathing
- fidgeting, clammy hands

If you have, then you are almost certainly shy. Virtually everybody is. There are very few teenagers or even adults come to that, who have not felt shy at one time or another. However, it is possible to overcome shyness successfully.

OVERCOMING SHYNESS

Everyone acts differently in the comfort of their own home because they feel safe and comforted by familiar surroundings. It's when you know you are going to have to go out and face new situations and meet people that the problems set in.

FEEL COMFORTABLE WITH WHOM YOU ARE

Take a good look at yourself. Think of the good points, both of your looks and personality. Everyone has some, even if they do think they are outnumbered by the bad! Stop feeling sorry for yourself and instead find a reason to feel good. This is the first and biggest hurdle to overcome shyness. It is easy!

THINK POSITIVE

If you think that nobody will want to talk to you, or that you look really ugly and that you are going to have a terrible time, then you more than likely will! If, on the other hand, you go with a slightly more optimistic outlook, even in the slight hope of enjoying yourself then you probably will. The power of positive thought can be amazing and being confident will give you a new sense of self.

DISGUISE YOUR SHYNESS WELL

Start to think of yourself as a bit of an actress. Take on a kind of alter ego, a Ms Glamour Queen and try to calm down the quivering wreck on the inside to radiate a calm, confident exterior. Remember the

last time you wilted with shyness? Next time you feel an attack coming on, take a deep breath and smile. You will fool everyone that you are actually enjoying yourself. Try to focus on and aim your smile at one other person in the room, preferably one who is on their own and looks as shy as you feel. By doing so, you will make them feel more comfortable and this will have the same effect on you.

WHAT YOUR BODY SAYS

Body language is a whole series of unspoken often subconscious signals given by the way you look, hold yourself and gesticulate. They can reveal your inner feelings.

Even if you feel shy, you can develop positive body language. Smiling, for example, is one of the simplest, most natural forms there is (although smiling inanely can look rather strange!). Smiling decreases your blood pressure and will make you feel better in a medical sense too. Here are a few more examples of both positive and negative body language. Perhaps you have been guilty of a few without knowing!

Positive Body Language:
- smiling
- placing hands relaxed on uncrossed knees
- keeping eye contact
- standing upright, facing the person you are speaking to

Shrinking Violets – The Killer Shyness

Negative Body Language:
- frowning
- crossing arms and legs tightly
- avoiding eye contact
- standing side on to the person you are speaking to
- holding hands to your face
- putting hands in front of your mouth
- hands in pockets
- fidgeting with rings, fingers or clothing
- hunched shoulders

If you do become conscious of doing any of these negative signs then try to change them. Otherwise, you may as well have a sign on your head saying 'I'm nervous' in neon colours and flashing lights!

By relaxing, you will look confident and so will give people an open invitation to approach you and get to know you better. Then, half the battle is already won.

STOP THINKING ABOUT YOURSELF

You might worry that everyone is looking at you, but they are not. They are far too busy thinking about themselves. They are probably just as nervous as you are. Notice other people or concentrate on anything at all, besides yourself. Try to look friendly as you are doing this. You don't want to make them feel even more uncomfortable, but instead you want to put them at ease; you will do this best by looking relaxed but friendly. You will then give them a chance to want to get to know what is beneath that calm exterior and discover the real you, instead of instantly frightening them off!

BE A PARTY ANIMAL

Parties are especially frightening situations. Take heed of all the above points. It is a perfect opportunity to put them all into practice!

Accepting an invitation to a party when you feel weak at the knees just thinking about it, may be one of the most difficult things you can do. It will almost certainly be one of the bravest as well. If you do force yourself to go, another part of the battle is won. You will get accustomed to the once-terrifying situation and you will probably even begin to enjoy it.

STRIKING UP A CONVERSATION

The easiest way to do this is to join in on a conversation that is already under way. Wait until a subject comes up that you can contribute to. Take a deep breath, clear your throat, swallow and talk.

Try not to be too concerned about yourself and don't be too conscious of the fact that your cheeks are bright red, that your voice is changing pitch and wandering as though you have been possessed and that your tongue is so dry that it feels like the Sahara desert has been emptied onto it!

Ask questions. Have a few icebreakers ready to throw in when the opportunity arises:

- What school/class are you in?
- How do you know the host/hostess?
- Do you know anyone else?
- Everyone loves to talk about themselves. Don't talk about yourself for too long as you could end up boring your audience silly! Try to appear interested in them instead. Make sure too, that the questions you ask require more than a simple 'yes' or 'no' in response. Also remember to answer any questions you are asked with another. Before you know it, you will be having a conversation. If not, then the person you are talking to is probably even shyer than you!

TALKING TO BOYS

If the person you are talking to happens to be a member of the opposite sex, then you may be just that little bit more nervous – especially if he has been the boy of your dreams for the past six months! Don't force yourself to become Ms Popular just to impress him. This may have the opposite effect as he might be intimidated by your confidence and back off completely. Don't worry, either, that you are nowhere near as pretty as your best friend. He's not talking to her, he's talking to you! Tastes vary. Just because you think your friend is gorgeous looking, it doesn't necessarily mean everyone else does. If you feel inferior to the life and soul of the party, then he probably will too and she is going to be last on his list of interests.

Boys are strange animals. Very often they don't notice new hairstyles, trendy clothes or make-up – and spots are something they themselves can't escape. It really is what's inside that counts. As long as you are yourself and you feel comfortable with that, then others will be too.

Boys are not really an alien life form. They're only human and are not always in control of situations either, although they may appear to be. What they may be doing is going for an Oscar nomination themselves!

Shy people very often don't speak up for themselves as much as they should, simply because they are too afraid. It is in your interest and it is extremely important to be able to speak your mind. It may seem quite insignificant, but just being able to say no to someone when you mean it could save you from an awful lot of trouble, especially with boys. If you disagree with something, say so. Make an effort not to be manipulated and forced into things you don't want to do. Stand up for yourself.

Overcoming shyness is not easy. It takes a far braver person to face up to their problems and try to change the way they are than one who ignores them and continues on the way they have always been. Shyness can dominate or even ruin your life if you let it. It can be a constant series of battles which you keep fighting with yourself for the rest of your life. However, the more you try to overcome shyness, the more you will succeed, until you get to that stage when you actually *look forward* to meeting new people! Ask your parents, friends or teachers what their solution is. They may be able to give you a few tips. Whatever you do, don't just sit back and wait for things to happen to you. Get out there and enjoy yourself while you make them happen. You are in control of your own destiny. It is all down to you and no one else, so what are you waiting for? Good luck!

SELF CONFIDENCE TEST

So you think you are fully in control? Then have a go at this little quiz to make sure!

You look in the mirror; what do you honestly see?
a) A blob of lard with spots
d) Just myself really

c) A girl of average height and build with average hair and a dash of acne
b) The most attractive girl I know

You are in a crowded room and a devastatingly handsome boy smiles right at you. What do you think?
c) He must think I am someone else
a) Either he's laughing at me or he has got trapped wind!
d) Oooh!! – He's nice! – and then smile back
b) Smile, wave frantically and scream 'What's your name, sexy? Come here often?'

How many good points do you have?
a) Did you say good?
c) I'm sure there must be some hidden well under this fat somewhere
d) A few but most of them you can't see
b) Where do you want me to start? Got 20 minutes to spare?

You are at a party with your leg in plaster when a boy asks you to dance. What do you say?
c) Nothing, you are both laughing too much
a) 'Very funny' then whack him with your crutches
b) Say yes and desperately try to shimmy sexily for an hour
d) 'Usually I'd jump at the chance. Fancy a go on my crutches instead?'

Someone passes you a genuine compliment. How do you respond?
a) 'How much did Mum and Dad pay you to say that?'
b) Thanks, I know
d) Thanks very much! So do you
c) Umm . . . really? Thanks

Add your score up and see how you did below.

Mostly a)
You are too cynical for your own good.

Mostly b)
Are you for real?!

Mostly c)
Plenty of potential but still bringing yourself down.

Mostly d)
Great! The perfect combination! You have obviously read this book inside out and back to front!

INDEX

Other books from Piccadilly Press's teenage list:

BOYS – A USER'S GUIDE
by Morag Prunty

"The witty presentation and the amusing cartoons make a very acceptable 'front' for such a sensitive subject. This book should be popular"
School Librarian

DON'T PICK ON ME
How to Handle Bullying
by Rosemary Stones

"At last someone has written clear and welcome advice for children on how to handle bullying"
Daily Mail

EVERYBODY ELSE DOES – WHY CAN'T I?
by Yvonne Coppard

Diary entries of Jennifer and her mother reveal their different views on life.

". . . The book is so unpretentiously tied in to teenage life that it is sure to find many readers"
School Librarian

I WAS A TEENAGE WORRIER
by Ros Asquith

"Unique, hilarious. It knocks the spots of anything else I've read for teenagers." The Bookseller

THE TEENAGE WORRIER'S FRIEND
by Ros Asquith

Letty Chubb, the teenage worrier, is back by popular demand – this time with a hilarious all-in-one fact-file, address book and diary.

KEEP OUT OF THE REACH OF PARENTS
A Teenager's Guide to Bringing Them Up
by John Farman

"John Farman has written a humorous and readable guide to likely bones of contention between parents and teenagers." Daily Mail

Just published:

THIRTEENSOMETHING
A Survivor's Guide
by Jane Goldman

Life's not easy when your thirteensomething, but this guide to being a teenager will make it an awful lot better.

STAYING COOL, SURVIVING SCHOOL
Secondary School Strategies
by Rosie Rushton

At last – a light-hearted but informative look at secondary school. Discover what really goes on there, and learn the survival strategies.